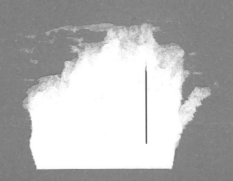

HEDGEHOGS

Sally Morgan

W

FRANKLIN WATTS

LONDON • SYDNEY

© 2005 Franklin Watts
First published in 2005
by Franklin Watts
96 Leonard Street
London EC2A 4XD

Franklin Watts Australia
45-51 Huntley Street
Alexandria NSW 2015

Produced for Franklin Watts by
White-Thomson Publishing Ltd
210 High Street
Lewes BN7 2NH

Editor: Rachel Minay
Designed by: Tinstar Design Ltd
Picture research: Morgan Interactive Ltd
Consultant: Frank Blackburn
Printed in: China

**British Library Cataloguing
in Publication Data**
A CIP catalogue record for this book is
available from the British Library.

ISBN: 0 7496 6069 4

Acknowledgements
The publishers would like to thank
the following for permission to
reproduce these photographs:

Ecoscene
4–5 (Robert Pickett), 6 (Chinch Gryniewicz),
11 (Steve Austin), 14 (Robert Pickett),
15 (Jamie Harron), 16, 20, 25 (Robert
Pickett), 26 (Robin Redfern), 28 (Martin
Lillicrap), 29 (Robert Pickett);

Nature Picture Library
FC, 1 (Niall Benvie), 7 (Ingo Arndt),
8 (Andrew Cooper), 9 (George McCarthy),
10 (Niall Benvie), 12 (Paul Hobson),
13 (Dietmar Nill), 17 (Fabio Liverani),
18 (Jim Hallett), 19 (Dominic Johnson),
21 (Dietmar Nill), 22 (Martin Smith),
23 (Dietmar Nill), 24 (Brian Lightfoot),
27 (Paul Hobson).

Every effort has been made to contact copyright
holders of any material reproduced in this book.
Any omissions will be rectified in subsequent
printings if notice is given to the publishers.

Contents

The hedgehog

The hedgehog is an easy animal to identify. It is covered in a thick coat of spines. When a hedgehog is attacked by another animal, it curls up into a tight ball with all its spines sticking out.

The hedgehog is a small grey-brown animal, with a long nose and round, bead-like eyes. Male and female hedgehogs look very similar. Their babies are called hoglets.

ANIMAL **FACTS**

▶ *An adult hedgehog is between 20 and 30 cm in length.*

▶ *It weighs between 1 and 2 kg.*

▶ *Hedgehogs live for two to three years, sometimes as long as five years.*

▶ *Hedgehogs are nocturnal; they are active at night.*

▶ *The Latin name for the hedgehog is Erinaceus europaeus.*

head

ears

eyes

nose

Hedgehogs are mammals

The hedgehog is a mammal. Female mammals produce milk for their young. Mammals do not usually produce large numbers of offspring. There is a lot of parental care involved in their upbringing.

spines

legs

The back of a hedgehog is covered in yellow-tipped spines.

Reproduction

Hedgehogs mate between March and July and the hoglets are born during the summer.

Hedgehog courtship is very noisy! The male and female hedgehogs circle around each other making snorting and snuffling sounds. After mating, the female hedgehog is pregnant for about five weeks. She makes a nest of grass and leaves under a hedge or tree root, or in an old rabbit hole. She gives birth to between three and seven hoglets.

Newborn hoglets look quite strange with their white spines sticking out of the pink skin.

The first brown spines have appeared but the eyes of this young hoglet are still closed.

First spines

The newborn hoglets don't have any spines when they are born and their skin is quite soft. However, within two hours of birth about 150 white spines push through the skin. These first spines are rubbery to the touch. Two days later the first proper spines start to appear. Young hoglets do not move far and they cannot roll up.

ANIMAL **FACTS**

▶ *Newborn hoglets are blind and deaf, and each weighs just 9 g. They stay close to their mother to keep warm.*

Growing up

For the first two weeks of their life, the hoglets do little more than eat. However, once their eyes and ears open they can see and hear what is going on.

At 14 days, hair starts to grow between their spines and the hoglets practise how to roll up, although they cannot do a complete roll yet. Their first teeth start to appear when they are about 21 days old. Now they are ready to follow their mother out of the nest.

Young hedgehogs look just like smaller versions of the adult hedgehogs.

This car has stopped to allow a family of hedgehogs to cross the road.

Feeding on milk

The hoglets feed on their mother's milk for about six to seven weeks. Then they are weaned. The mother feeds them less milk and lets them eat solid food such as worms. Once they are eating the same food as the adults they leave their mother and live on their own.

ANIMAL **FACTS**

▶ *Only one out of every four hoglets survives until its first birthday. Many hoglets are killed by predators or die from disease.*

Living in the countryside

Hedgehogs are found across Britain. Most live in woodland, hedgerows and farmland where there are plenty of hiding places. They do not like wide open spaces, such as large fields or moorland, as there is nowhere to hide.

Woodland homes

The favourite habitat of hedgehogs is open woodland. In these woodlands the trees are widely spaced and there are plenty of plants growing on the floor of the wood. Hedgehogs often wander around the countryside following the line of hedgerows. The undergrowth in woodlands and hedgerows provides plenty of food, and places to hide and build nests.

This hedgehog is walking through some open woodland.

Territories

Each hedgehog lives in a particular area called a territory. Hedgehogs have quite large territories for their size. A male has a territory of about 200,000 to 350,000 sq m while a female's territory is slightly smaller. They find all their food within the territory.

Rather than walk across the middle of a field, a hedgehog will move around the edges, staying under the cover of trees.

Living in cities

Hedgehogs have moved into cities and towns where they can be found in gardens and parks. They have got used to living close to people.

Visiting gardens

Hedgehogs are useful visitors to the garden as they eat many pests such as slugs and snails. Hedgehogs visit several gardens in an evening. Some people try to attract hedgehogs to their garden by putting out food (such as cat food) on a saucer.

Sometimes hedgehogs are seen in gardens during the day.

Urban hedgehogs may be seen scuttling across pavements and roads at night.

Dangers to hedgehogs

Towns and cities can be dangerous places for hedgehogs. Each year more than 100,000 hedgehogs are killed on British roads. Some hedgehogs are poisoned in gardens when they eat slugs that have eaten slug pellets, or when they eat the slug pellets themselves.

Hedgehogs usually sleep during the day and they can be harmed by strimmers, which are used to cut undergrowth and long grass. It is important for gardeners to check piles of leaves before burning them in autumn, as a hedgehog may be sleeping at the bottom of the pile.

ANIMAL **FACTS**

▶ *Some injured hedgehogs are cared for by people who run small hedgehog hospitals.*

Spines

Hedgehogs are one of only a few mammals to have spines. Their spines cover their neck, back and sides. Spines provide hedgehogs with great protection against their predators.

Spines are hairs

Spines are really toughened hairs. They are strong but flexible, so they can bend. Adults have about 5,000 spines and each one ends in a needle-sharp point. At the skin end of the spine there is a ball-like root and a muscle that can pull the spine upright. As the hedgehog rolls tighter, the spines stick out more. There are softer hairs between the spines and over the rest of the body.

The spines are about 2 to 3 cm long. The ends are yellow-brown in colour.

Fleas and lice

A large number of fleas and lice live between the spines of a hedgehog. If you pick up a hedgehog you soon see fleas running over your hand!

Nobody is sure why hedgehogs smear saliva over their spines. It may be to clean them or remove fleas.

Movement

Hedgehogs have four stout legs, each of which ends in five toes.

Bones are moved by muscles

The hedgehog has an internal skeleton made up of many bones, which are attached to muscles. When a muscle contracts or gets shorter, it pulls on the bone and moves it.

ANIMAL **FACTS**

▶ *Only four of the hedgehog's five toes touch the ground. The fifth toe is much smaller and is positioned higher on the foot. This means that footprints of hedgehogs only show four toes.*

Hedgehogs can climb up and down steps in gardens in their search for food.

*Hedgehogs can swim
across streams and ponds.*

Getting around

Most of the time a hedgehog shuffles around with
its nose to the ground, trying to find food. However,
hedgehogs can run. When a hedgehog runs, it holds
its legs quite straight and its body off the ground. They
are surprisingly good climbers and can get over low
walls around gardens. If they have to, hedgehogs can
swim. However, they may have trouble getting out of
deep ponds or swimming pools and drown.

Hedgehogs are nocturna

Hedgehogs are nocturnal animals. This means they sleep during the day and come out at night to feed.

Hedgehogs come out at night

Hedgehogs emerge at dusk to feed. They cannot see much because it is dark and they rely on their other senses to find their way around. They are active all night.

ANIMAL **FACTS**

▶ Hedgehogs can travel up to 3 km during the night. Male hedgehogs walk further than females because they can walk faster. A male hedgehog looks for a female to mate with, as well as for food.

This hedgehog is sniffing for food in a garden.

Hedgehogs sleep during the day

A hedgehog spends the daylight hours asleep in its nest under a hedgerow or in the woodland undergrowth. Urban hedgehogs may sleep in gardens, sheltering at the back of the flower border or under a hedge.

Woodland hedgehogs build their nests in the tangled undergrowth of plants. The nest is made of grass and leaves and can be constructed very quickly. A hedgehog uses its nest for just a few days and then it moves on and builds a new one or finds an abandoned one.

Hedgehogs search for leaves and bits of grass to make into a nest.

Senses

The hedgehog's senses of hearing and smell are excellent but its sight is very poor.

Sniffing for food

A hedgehog relies on its sense of smell to find food. Often hedgehogs run while they are sniffing as this helps them to pick up scents more easily. They can smell people from several metres away and they can detect food buried up to 2 cm deep in the ground. A hedgehog also relies on its sense of smell to find its way around and to identify other hedgehogs.

ANIMAL **FACTS**

▶ *One blind hedgehog was observed to travel more than 1 km each night, walking from its nest on a golf course to a number of gardens to feed.*

The hedgehog has a long snout. The snout is surrounded by long stiff hairs, called whiskers, that are sensitive to touch.

A hedgehog finds most of its food using its sense of smell. This hedgehog has found a slug.

Hearing

A hedgehog's hearing is good enough to be able to detect small animals such as insects and worms moving along the ground. Hedgehogs can also hear predators approaching.

Poor eyesight

Hedgehogs are active at night and have small eyes, so they do not rely on their sight. Blind hedgehogs can find their way around with ease, proving that sight is not important to them.

science LINKS

How good are you at finding objects with your eyes closed? Try this experiment with a friend. Place a blindfold over your eyes. A friend then positions objects on a table in front of you. You have to find the objects they call out.

Hedgehog food

Hedgehogs belong to a group of mammals called Insectivora, the insect-eaters. Although they eat a lot of insects, they eat other foods too.

Hedgehogs eat animal foods

Hedgehogs eat almost any type of invertebrate that they find. Invertebrates are animals that do not have a backbone and they include caterpillars, beetles, snails, slugs, worms and spiders. Sometimes hedgehogs eat vertebrate animals (animals with backbones) such as frogs, toads and lizards. They may scavenge for the remains of dead animals and sometimes they take eggs from birds' nests on the ground.

On some islands, hedgehogs eat the eggs of seabirds.

science **LINKS**

Hedgehogs have 32 small pointed teeth. Using a mirror, look at your teeth. How many teeth do you have? Can you see the four different types of teeth in your mouth – incisors, canines, premolars and molars? Incisors are small teeth at the front of the mouth. You have four canines behind them. The large teeth at the back of your mouth are your premolars and molars.

Hedgehogs eat plant foods

Hedgehogs eat foods from plants too. They like to eat fallen fruit, such as apples, in autumn and also feed on seeds, berries, grass and leaves.

The hedgehog uses its pointed teeth to crunch through a snail's shell.

Hedgehogs have enemies

Hedgehogs have a number of enemies, so their spines are an important defence.

Ball of spines

The hedgehog defends itself by rolling into a tight ball at the first sign of danger. The spines stick out, making it difficult for most animals to pick the hedgehog up, although a few foxes and dogs have learnt how to do it. A hedgehog also makes a lot of noise when threatened, squealing loudly like a pig.

When a hedgehog rolls up, it tucks its head right under its body so that it is protected.

ANIMAL **FACTS**

▶ *Some foxes have learnt how to get a hedgehog to unroll by urinating on it, while others drop the hedgehog in water to make it uncurl!*

The fox is one of the hedgehog's main enemies. Many hoglets are eaten by foxes before their spines have grown.

Predators

A few predators, such as badgers and eagles, try to force open a rolled-up hedgehog. Badgers, for example, use their strong claws to rip open the hedgehog's body. For this reason, the badger is one of the hedgehog's main predators. Some badgers can smell a hibernating hedgehog and dig it out.

science LINKS

The hedgehog is an important part of the woodland food chain. Plants are called producers. Animals that eat plants are called primary consumers. Animals that eat primary consumers are called secondary consumers. A simple woodland food chain is plant – snail – hedgehog – badger.

Surviving winter

Hedgehogs cannot find enough food in winter, so they go into a deep sleep called hibernation.

Underneath this pile of leaves is a hibernating hedgehog.

Hibernation

During the autumn hedgehogs prepare for winter by eating a lot of food. They have to build up their body fat. In November, when it gets colder, a hedgehog makes an extra-thick nest under a pile of leaves. It uses leaves and moss to keep the rain out and trap the heat. It crawls into its nest and goes into a deep sleep, in which its heart beats very slowly and its body temperature falls.

ANIMAL **FACTS**

▸ *An adult hedgehog weighs about 1 kg in spring. It eats lots of food in summer and autumn, and by the time it is ready to hibernate it weighs twice as much, about 2 kg. A young hedgehog has to weigh at least 500 g if it is to survive hibernation.*

Some people build or buy a hibernation box for hedgehogs and put it in their garden.

During the winter the hedgehog uses up its fat stores and loses a lot of weight. It wakes up again in April. Sometimes hedgehogs wake up in the middle of winter and emerge to find food.

Many hedgehogs die in winter hibernation if they are ill or underweight. If the winter is mild and there is plenty of food around, hedgehogs may not hibernate.

SCIENCE LINKS

A hedgehog's normal body temperature is about 35°C. When it hibernates, this falls to about 4°C. Do you know the normal body temperature of a human? Ask an adult to help you find out your temperature using a thermometer.

Hedgehog stories

Carrying fruits on spines

About two thousand years ago a Roman writer called Pliny wrote that hedgehogs carried fruits around, impaled on their spines. This may be partly true since hedgehogs often catch things on their spines by accident, but usually they carry food in their mouths. And how could they get the fruits off their spines again!

A sign of spring?

The Romans believed that the behaviour of the hedgehog could tell them when spring was coming. If a hedgehog comes out of its nest at night on the 2nd February and there is a clear moon, it knows that there are just six more weeks of winter. It goes back to its nest to sleep until mid-March.

Hedgehog facts

Hedgehog family

The European hedgehog is found in western and northern Europe. There are 17 species or types of hedgehog and they are found in Europe, Africa and Asia. They include moonrats, shrew-hedgehogs, long-eared hedgehogs and desert hedgehogs. All the hedgehogs belong to a large group of mammals called insectivores. Insectivores are small mammals with long, narrow snouts. Other insectivores include shrews and moles.

MAIN FEATURES OF THE HEDGEHOG

- *Hedgehogs are mammals.*
- *Hedgehogs belong to a group of mammals called insectivores (the insect-eaters).*
- *Hedgehogs eat both plant and animal foods.*
- *Baby hedgehogs are called hoglets.*
- *An adult hedgehog lives on its own in an area called a territory.*
- *Hedgehogs usually hibernate in winter.*

Hedgehog websites

Epping Forest Hedgehog Rescue
www.thehedgehog.co.uk/garden.htm
Website that provides facts about hedgehogs and suggests ways of attracting them into the garden.

British Hedgehog Preservation Society
www.software-technics.com/bhps/
Website that gives information about the work of the Society as well as advice for looking after orphaned hoglets.

Note to parents and teachers
Every effort has been made by the publishers to ensure that these websites are suitable for children; that they are of the highest educational value, and that they contain no inappropriate or offensive material. However, because of the nature of the Internet, it is impossible to guarantee that the contents of these sites will not be altered. We strongly advise that Internet access is supervised by a responsible adult.

Glossary

food chain feeding relationships between different organisms, for example slugs are eaten by hedgehogs and hedgehogs are eaten by badgers

habitat the place where an animal lives

hoglet a young hedgehog

mammal an animal that usually gives birth to live young. The female mammal produces milk for her young

mate reproduce

moorland a type of habitat found in upland areas with low-growing plants such as heather, and no trees

nocturnal animals that are nocturnal are active at night and rest during the day

pest an animal that does harm to garden plants, crops or other animals

predator an animal that hunts other animals

pregnant a female animal is pregnant when she has a baby or babies developing inside her

saliva the fluid produced in the mouth to help the chewing and swallowing of food

scavenge feed on dead and decaying food and food in rubbish

snout the nose and mouth which stick out from the face of some animals

strimmer a garden tool used to cut down vegetation

territory the range or area of land in which an animal lives

undergrowth the tangle of low-growing plants under trees

urinating releasing urine (the water passed out of the body of an animal) from the body

weaning changing a baby animal from a milk diet to foods eaten by adult animals

Index